LifeCycles

Egg to Chicken

Camilla de la Bédoyère

QED Publishing

First published in the UK in 2009 by
QED Publishing
A Quarto Group company
226 City Road
London EC1V 2TT

www.qed-publishing.co.uk

A catalogue record for this book is available
from the British Library.

ISBN 978 1 84835 224 7

Printed and bound in China

Author Camilla de la Bédoyère
Editor Angela Royston
Designer and Picture Researcher Melissa Alaverdy

Publisher Steve Evans
Creative Director Zeta Davies
Managing Editor Amanda Askew

Words in **bold** are explained in the glossary on page 22.

Picture credits
(t=top, b=bottom, l=left, r=right, c=centre, fc=front cover)
Corbis 1t Holger Winkler/AB/zefa, 1b Craig Holmes/Loop Images, 5t Martin
Harvey, 6–7 Craig Holmes/Loop Images, 11b Holger Winkler/AB/zefa
Getty Images 10–11 Georgette Douwma, 11t Bob Elsdale, 12 Dorling
Kindersley, 15b Tara Moore, 17t Jane Burton, 17b GK Hart/
Vikki Hart, 18 Klaus Nigge
Photolibrary Group 9t John Cancalosi, 13 Harald Lange, 14 Andre
Maslennikov, 20–21 Harald Lange
Shutterstock 2t iofoto, 4b Dee Hunter, 4–5 Valio, 5b JanJar, 6b JanJar,
6t Gelpi, 8 Craig Hanson, 8 Craig Hanson, 9b Babusi Octavian Florentin,
15t AGphotographer, 16b Saied Shahin Kiya, 16c Saied Shahin Kiya, 16t Saied
Shahin Kiya, 19 Babusi Octavian Florentin, 20l Jozsef Szasz-Fabian,
22–23 Vasyl Helevachuk, 24 Saied Shahin Kiya

Contents

What is a chicken?

A chicken is a type of bird. All birds have feathers and wings, and all birds lay eggs.

Feathers help birds to fly, and to stay warm and dry. Flying takes a lot of energy, so birds need to eat often.

⇩ Birds have mouths called beaks or bills, but no teeth.

⇧ Gulls spread their wings and feathery tails when they fly.

4

Not all birds can fly. Ostriches have wings, but cannot fly. Ostriches are the world's largest birds. Some are more than 2 metres tall.

Ostrich egg

⇧ Ostrich feathers are long, soft and fluffy.

⇨ One ostrich egg weighs the same as 24 hen eggs.

Hen egg

The story of a chicken

There are more chickens in the world than any other type of bird.

A hen is a female chicken. A male chicken is called a rooster or a cockerel. A chick is a baby chicken.

Chicks begin their lives as eggs. The story of how an egg grows into an adult chicken is called a **life cycle**.

⇨ A chicken goes through three stages in its life cycle.

Chick

2

1

Egg

3

Adult chicken

Making a nest

Hens start laying eggs when they are around six months old. First, they need a **nest** to lay the eggs in.

Most birds build their nests in trees. They may use twigs, grass or moss.

⇦ Ospreys build huge nests of twigs in trees and on rooftops.

⇨ The smallest nests are built by hummingbirds.

Hens build their nests on the ground. They find somewhere dry and quiet, and use straw or grass to make the nest.

⇩ Hens build their nests in barns or hen houses, where they are warm and safe.

The eggs are laid

A hen usually lays one egg a day. The eggs will only grow into chicks if the hen has already **mated** with a rooster.

When a rooster wants to mate, he crows loudly. As they mate, the rooster **fertilizes** the hen's eggs.

⇦ A rooster also crows to tell other males to stay away.

⇨Roosters are bigger than hens and they have longer tail feathers.

⇩The hen starts to lay her eggs a day after mating.

Only fertilized eggs can grow into chicks. A group of eggs is called a clutch.

Brooding

When the hen has laid all her eggs in the nest, she sits on them to keep them warm. This is called **brooding**, and it is an important job.

The hen has to sit on her clutch while the chicks grow. If the eggs become cold, the chicks stop growing.

⇨ A brooding hen spreads her feathers over the eggs.

⇧ A nesting box makes a safe, warm home for hens and their eggs.

The hen turns the eggs from time to time to keep them warm all over.

Inside the egg

All bird eggs are protected by a hard **shell**. Inside each fertilized egg, a tiny chick is growing.

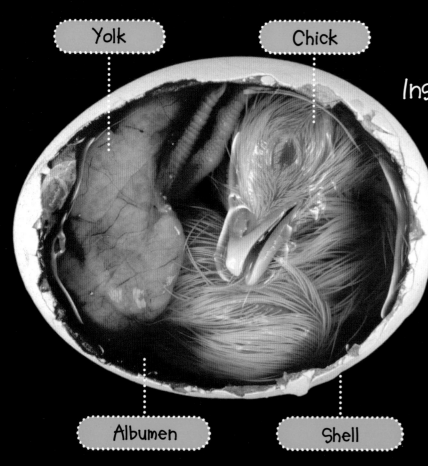

Yolk

Chick

Albumen

Shell

Inside the egg, the chick gets food from the yellow **yolk** and **albumen**. The albumen is the clear liquid that we call the white of the egg. It protects the chick and keeps it warm.

⇦ Chicks need air to breathe. The larger end of the egg holds an air space.

Hens lay eggs even when they have not mated. The eggs we eat have not been fertilized. They don't have chicks inside them.

⇧ Most chicken egg shells are brown, white or cream.

⇨ Chicken eggs are easy to cook, and good to eat!

The eggs hatch

After growing for about three weeks, the young chicks are ready to break out of their eggs. This is called **hatching**.

Each chick has a sharp point on their top beak, called an egg-tooth.

3

2

1

⇧ It uses its body to push the shell apart.

⇦ It chips a hole all round the shell.

⇦ The chick uses its egg-tooth to crack a hole in the shell.

4

⇐ Then it climbs out of the shell.

The newly hatched chick cheeps loudly. It is tired and its feathers are wet. Once the feathers have dried, they become fluffy.

5

⇒ Soon all the chicks have hatched out!

Life as a chick

The hen looks after her newly hatched chicks. She keeps them warm under her wings.

When they are just two weeks old, the chicks can leave the barn or hen house and explore outside.

⇦ Newly hatched chicks stay close to their mother.

18

Chicks and chickens like to scratch around in the dirt, looking for tasty worms or bugs to eat.

⇨Chickens do not have teeth, so they cannot chew their food. They swallow it whole instead.

Growing and changing

The chicks grow into adults in just a few months. Glossy feathers grow in place of the soft, fluffy feathers.

The chicks grow red, fleshy combs on top of their heads. The combs help to keep them cool.

⇧ A hen that is less than one year old is called a pullet.

Soon the young hens will start to lay eggs. When a hen mates, a new life cycle begins.

⇩Roosters have colourful feathers and grow larger combs than hens.

Comb

Glossary

Albumen
The white of an egg.

Brooding
When a hen sits on her eggs to keep them warm.

Comb
The soft, red skin on top of a chicken's head.

Fertilize
When a special cell from a male joins with a female's egg to form a new living thing.

Hatching
When a chick breaks out of its egg.

Life cycle
The story of how an animal changes from birth to death, and how it produces young.

Mated
When a male and a female have come together to produce young.

Nest
A safe place that birds make where they can lay their eggs.

Shell
The hard outside of an egg. It protects the chick inside.

Yolk
The yellow part of an egg. The yolk is food for the chick inside the egg.

Index

Notes for parents and teachers

🐔 Look through the book and talk about the pictures. Read the captions and ask questions about other things in the photographs that have not been mentioned in the text.

🐔 Find out more about birds by watching them in the wild. Help children to use a guidebook to identify different birds. Remind them that nests and eggs should never be approached or disturbed.

🐔 Science at home. Carry out some simple experiments with a hen's egg. Try rolling it on a smooth surface and watch how it moves. See what happens when you float an egg in water (the freshest eggs sink). Open the egg and identify the different parts. Hard boil an egg and talk about the way heat has changed its contents.

🐔 Be prepared for questions about human life cycles. There are plenty of books available for this age group that can help you give age-appropriate explanations.

🐔 Talking about a child's family helps them to link life processes to their own experience. Drawing simple family trees, looking at photos and talking to grandparents are fun ways to engage young children.